Babies Having Babies

Young Girls Interrupted

PEGGY HATCHET

ISBN: 1517001919
ISBN-13: 9781517001919

DEDICATION

To teen mothers…hold your head up.

Table of Contents

PROLOGUE

This teen-pregnancy phenomenon dates as far back as the 16th century when girls were having babies with the advent of their menstrual cycles. It was in part due to various customs and traditions; as well as the thinking that women were not worthy of basic human considerations.

The Women's Liberation Movement came along and afforded women and girls control over their own bodies i.e. their basic human rights, though remnants of chauvinistic attitudes still remained. In other words, girls were (and are) still viewed as "pieces of meat" to be devoured through sexual exploits.

Unfortunately, girls began viewing themselves as tarts and sex objects—seeing themselves as "things" to be handled by anyone giving them attention.

Television, magazines, and music outlets perpetuate this thinking by representing women as naked video vixens, who appear as having no shame or morals. Though the girls who dance in these videos do it as a paid job assignment; they have no idea of the long-term affects their performance has on women and how they are viewed and treated around the globe.

Unlike centuries earlier, girls are no longer shackled to oppressive customs that subjugate them to being "baby-makers" and maids, with no other options.

Ironically, now that women and girls are not subject to demeaning dispositions, they now oppress themselves by their own thinking and actions. Young girls are not forced to follow some weird tradition by having to marry and have kids at 12 and 13 years old. Today, young girls engage in sexual acts out of misplaced ideas of love, which they don't understand. They become pregnant as a side-effect of their confusion.

Oh...To Be Young

I t's the beginning of spring; and all life is vibrant with color, beauty, and energy. Birds sing while perched on tree limbs outside open windows. Squirrels dart in and out of hiding, while butterflies dance merrily amid wonderfully fragranced flower gardens. Yes! Everyone loves spring. However, spring also represents reproduction, newness or creation of life.

Only a few more weeks before summer vacation, when parents allow their sons use of the family car; and he hurries across town to pick up his girlfriend and heads to the popular hang-out spot—where any...and everything goes; kids make bad choices, learning hard lessons as a result.

Kids from school gather to drink beer; smoke pot; play loud music; indulge in sexual activity. They say *it's all part of growing up*—trial and error, rebellion, and honest mistakes.

Parents are outraged when they learn of their kids' actions. They don't mean to be harsh. Parents were once kids too; they want to shield their own kids from their mistakes.

Many times parents' behavior as teens was identical to their kids' current behavior. The only thing missing is information and proper use of it. Information gives you choices that you otherwise wouldn't have.

Some people say, *"You're wasting your time. Kids don't listen."*

Well, a parent's responsibility is NOT to make kids listen; but to give them the information in a way that they at least hear it. This way, they have a choice between early and reckless sex and the challenges of abstinence—neither of which are easy to endure.

Innocent infatuation or puppy love is natural to the human experience. And both are connected to hormonal activity, where sex is an impulsive factor. There is nothing wrong with sexual attraction. Acting on it is another thing.

The key is to guide this impulse in kids by giving them truthful information.

Growing up is 5% instruction and 95% experiment

Kids…teens…young adults—whatever you prefer…it's time to take responsibility for your actions.

In fairness to parents, they do strive to make sure their daughters are not engaging in careless and premature sex. Their methods may be outdated or unconventional, nevertheless, mothers can relate to their daughters' sexual challenges; and they want to help them. However, it's very difficult for mother and daughter to talk about sex.

On the other hand, it's also fair to say that all kids suffer from the "forbidden fruit" syndrome that comes with "don't do that". Nevertheless, that's no excuse for kids to make poor decisions. In the Internet age, they can find information on literally any topic. There's no logical excuse for not knowing in 2015.

CONSEQUENCES OF ENGAGING IN CARELESS SEX:

1. SEXUALLY TRANSMITTED DISEASE (STD)
2. STERILITY CAUSED BY GENITAL DISEASE
3. FEMALE AILMENTS CAUSED BY ROUGH INTERCOURSE
4. UNWANTED PREGNANCY

It's natural to think or believe "It will never happen to me." This is a dangerous attitude to have. You'll be in the middle of self-created confusion when it does happen to you.

It's unfortunate that so many kids believe themselves to be immune to being infected by sexually transmitted disease. They argue that "a person has to participate in sex all the time to become infected—kinda' like a prostitute or something." The facts disagree with this argument. **All it takes is one "infected" encounter** to become infected with an STD.

This is not only true for Syphilis; it's true for all diseases that are transmitted through sexual intercourse. In fact, the number of cases affecting kids 15 to 19 years of age is staggering. It can easily be you. These numbers are per year.

Disease	Gender	Age	# of Cases
Chlamydia	Female	15 – 19	317,724
Gonorrhea	Female	15 – 19	47,777
Primary & Secondary Syphilis	Female	15 – 19	204
Total			365,705

U.S. Department of Health and Human Services, Centers for Disease Control and Prevention, National Center for HIV, STD and TB Prevention (NCHSTP), Division of STD/HIV Prevention, Sexually Transmitted Disease Morbidity for selected STDs by age, race/ethnicity and gender 1996-2013, CDC WONDER Online Database.

Have you ever considered the rate of disease-transmission among sexually active teens, who have no idea that they're infected, or that they're infecting others?

STDs are passed simply by one-at-a-time encounters. This one gives it to that one; that one gives it to the other one; the other one gives it to someone; so forth and so on.

Couples break up; and they become involved with other people with whom they exchange body fluids. This is what makes the issue of careless sex so grave. In cases of HIV it's a matter of life and death.

Let's look at some of these diseases and break down the health risks of each one.

Chlamydia – A common STD that can infect both men and women. It can cause serious, permanent damage to women's reproductive system, making it gravely difficult to get pregnant later in life.

You can get Chlamydia by having vaginal, anal, or oral sex with someone who has it. If your sex partner is male you can still get Chlamydia even if he doesn't ejaculate.

How can you reduce your risk of getting *Chlamydia?*

The only way to avoid STDs is to not have vaginal, oral, or anal sex.

Yes. That last statement is unrealistic, in terms of actually following through with this type of discipline. No one expects you to NEVER have sex. The issue at hand involves *careless* and *random* sex because "everybody is doing it."

Realistically, sex is a very natural part of human interaction. And like everything else, it becomes dangerous when abused. Marriage…and faithfulness to your partner are safeguards against STDs. Or—at least—they should be.

Spouses who are faithful to their marriages and couples who are exclusive in their relationships face no real threat of contracting an STD. Their chances of having it are reduced to maybe having a case (you didn't know about) from a prior sexual relationship. Therefore, it's recommended that partners get physicals and share findings of any irregularities with each other.

The question is: **who cares enough about their physical wellbeing to take the necessary steps to safeguard against STDs?**

Do kids have the wherewithal to abstain from reckless pre-marital sex? If not, do you care enough about yourself to protect yourself? Or will you become one of the statistics generating from the CDC (Center for Disease Control) each year? You decide.

Some parents from the "old school" as you call it believe if you're under 18, you should still be a virgin. I won't attempt to tell you what to do. What do YOU think you should do?

Gonorrhea – is a sexually transmitted disease that affects both men and women. It can cause infections in the genitals, rectum, and throat. It's a very common infection, especially among young people ages 15 – 24.

Gonorrhea is spread by having vaginal, anal, or oral sex with someone who has it. A pregnant woman can give gonorrhea to her baby during childbirth.

Primary & Secondary Syphilis – is an STD that can cause long-term complications if not treated correctly. Symptoms in adults are divided into stages: primary, secondary, latent, and late syphilis.

You can get syphilis by direct contact with syphilis sores during vaginal, anal, or oral sex. Sores can be found on the penis, vagina, and anus, in the rectum, or on the lips and in the mouth. Syphilis can also be spread from an infected mother to her unborn baby.

Syphilis is called "the great imitator" because it has so many possible symptoms, many of which look like symptoms from other diseases.

The painless syphilis sore that you would get after you are first infected can be confused for an ingrown hair, zipper cut, or other seemingly harmless bump.

The non-itchy body rash that develops during the second stage of syphilis can show up on the palms of your hands and soles of your feet, all over your body, or in just a few places. You could also be infected with syphilis and have very mild symptoms or none at all.

Sounds scary, doesn't it? Well it should. Your body is not a vehicle. You can't go and get other parts once you permanently damage the ones you have.

Teen pregnancy – One of the oldest marvels of the human race. Girls have been having babies as early as age 12 (or whenever their menstrual cycle begins) for centuries. But why? She's still growing up at that age herself! Anyway…

You may think you're so in love; and you think he's the one for you; and he will never leave you. But you're both only 15! What do you know about love…or the sacrifice that having a baby requires? I'll answer that… "Nothing."

Life is always in springtime when you're young. Fun. Fun. And more fun. Enjoy it! Don't waste your youthful energy indulging in reckless sex. Do you know the purpose of sex?

Sexual energy is like angry energy. You have to use it in a positive, productive way. Join a dance class; an art class; start a book club or join one; learn to sew, knit, or crochet. Do anything to release sexual energy in a creative, productive way. Otherwise, run-away hormones gain control of your life; you become loose without realizing it.

Pregnant at 15

Y ou're scared and suddenly feel all alone. This month your menstrual cycle is late, very late. The month is almost gone and not as much as a spot.

The fact that your cycle is late is not as scary as thinking about what your parents will do—if you ARE with child. All kinds of thoughts run through your mind. Who can you tell? Is there anyone who will listen and not judge you?

Though you may not want to, maybe the first person you should tell your mother. Yes. She'll be shocked, hurt, and even disappointed. But she'll get over it. Even your mother was a young girl once; and she has made some poor choices of her own. She'll understand; and she won't judge you.

On the flip side of that, you now have to take ownership of your actions. You're the one who decided to engage in reckless sex. Now, you're simply experiencing the consequences of your actions. It's life. Life is <u>always</u> fair.

You hope you're just late and everything will go back to normal. Maybe so. Then you can learn this very valuable lesson: *You get what you give.*

Sex is not a plaything. It is the method by which humans populate the earth; become fruitful; and multiply. So when you get pregnant, guess what. You're supposed to. The only way to escape that possibility before you're ready is to NOT have sex.

Well…so much for wishful thinking. You find out you're really pregnant. You go weeks without telling anyone, except your boyfriend. When you tell him, he stops calling or coming by, you refuse to leave your room; you stop socializing altogether. The truth is your boyfriend isn't ready. You aren't ready; your parents aren't ready. Nobody is ready for a baby. Everything in your life dramatically shifts.

Your body is changing. You wish you could go back and make a different choice. But you have to live with the one you made.

Hormones are changing and you cry when the phone rings!

You're gaining weight and not just in your stomach. It's real. You're going to be a mother; and your body is changing to accommodate the growing baby inside you. Your body will do what it has to do to support not one, but two lives—yours and the baby's. Strange, huh?

You're 15, barely out of elementary school, and pregnant! Now is one of the few times you really want to be a kid.

YOUR RELATIONSHIP WITH YOUR PARENTS ENTERS ANOTHER PHASE

Tension is natural at this time. This is a new dynamic. None of you have had this experience together on this level. It's a highly stressful time for everyone, especially your mother.

It's great when teen mothers are fortunate enough to have family support allowing them to finish school.

When that's the case, "good old mom" is the one who gets up with the baby at night. So...yes. Your mom will feel the highest level of stress.

Every mom has high hopes and great expectations for their daughter. Whenever anything interferes with that ideal, mothers tend to blame themselves when things go wrong.

Get used to it. Things will be different for a while; maybe even from now on. You can never go back to being "daddy's little" girl. You're on your way to being a mother.

If your mother is quieter than usual at the dinner table, it's because she's thinking, trying to digest that fact that her *little girl* is not so little anymore.

Maybe she's dealing with the reality of becoming a grandmother ten years ahead of time. It's a lot for the mother of a 15-year-old to have to accept.

In some cases, your mom and dad may start arguing a lot. Each blaming the other for not being around or not doing enough.

Quiet and helpless pain rests in your father's eyes. He can't even look at you anymore. You think he won't look at you because he despises you for getting pregnant, despite all the trust he had in you to use the advice he gave you.

But he doesn't despise you. You're his little girl; he loves you. Like you, he has to adjust to you going from changing clothes to go to the mall, to changing diapers—to care for a child. That's a huge change.

Maybe he can't bear to look at you because every time he does, he blames himself—thinking he should have done something to protect you from this part of life. Most parents' daily routine is so cluttered that they go into shock when a part of life happens that they're not ready for.

This is not the time to retaliate against your parents. It's not the time to catch an attitude because you believe someone else has one. None of this is their fault. They're reacting to a part of life that happened to soon for you.

Everything is different. Nothing is the same. This is an adjustment for everybody, especially your parents. They have to endure criticism from friends and neighbors who question their parenting skills by asking, *"Where were her parents? How could this happen right under their noses?"*

Through it all; despite all the criticism and passing of judgment, nothing could ever cause your parents to stop loving you. You will disappoint them; they may even cry when you're not looking; you will have disagreements and differences of opinion. That's okay. You're supposed to have an independent thought and point of view. However, nothing should ever pierce the bond between parent and child...nothing.

~ You'll understand that when you have your own ~

FACE THE HARD TRUTH...

Just remember. None of this would be happening but for the choices you made. Your choices don't make you a bad person... hard-headed maybe, but not bad. You may be 15, but you made a 35-year-old decision. Now it's time to put on your big-girl shoes and deal with the big-girl choice you made.

You have to be available to your baby 24 hours a day

Motherhood Is Forever

R emember your first baby doll? How you kept it with
you all the time, even when you slept? Psychologists
believe the baby-doll concept prepares little girls for
motherhood. That may be true. It certainly would explain
the consistency, when dealing with teenage pregnancy.

Truth is…

Dolls are not real. They support a fantasy, make-believe.
In reality, though, it's better to have a doll. They don't cry at
random times throughout the night; you don't have to
change their diapers or feed them.

With dolls, you can put them away when you get tired.
Babies are different. They need constant care and attention.
You will not belong to yourself anymore. For the rest of
your life, you belong to your child.

Whatever he or she needs, you have to make it happen.
Whether it's feeding them at three in the morning or
rocking them back to sleep at midnight, you still have to
report to work…tired and rundown.

Children are wonderful! Everybody on the planet is
someone's child and had to be taken care of. So this is not
an effort to say having children is a bad thing. But you do
need to understand that having children is serious.
Children are forever; and so is motherhood.

Just think about your relationship with your mother. It's ongoing, right? Well you can expect the same thing when you become a mother. You don't grow out of it; the role doesn't expire; **motherhood is forever.**

No matter your age, lifestyle, or religious persuasion, your mother will always be there for you. She's on call 24 hours a day. Nothing is off limits when it comes to her children. Guess what. That's the general pattern for most, if not all, mothers. You're no different.

It's clear that when you have children, you no longer have the option of being the focus. Your infant child, who depends on you for everything, becomes your main focus. You become second.

This will last for all of your child's growing years and into college. Can you imagine putting your life on hold at 15? And keeping it on hold for the next 20 or 21 years—maybe longer?

Even after your child graduates college or marries, your role as mother does not end. You will be connected for the rest of your lives. That's not a bad thing. It's just a reality.

ADOPTION OR ABORTION DOESN'T CHANGE MOTHERHOOD

Twenty girls were surveyed, asked whether they believed their role as a mother ended with adoption. Eighteen of them said they are no longer mothers. And when asked the same question about abortion, all twenty believed they cannot be considered mothers, after having an abortion.

It's understandable that young girls, taking steps to avoid having a baby too early in life, don't want to be characterized as a *mother*. The whole point of an abortion or adoption is to NOT be a mother. We get it.

It's okay that you don't want to be a mother right now; and you don't want to see yourself as one. There's nothing wrong with feeling that way.

However, the problem is not whether you keep the baby. The problem begins when you engage in the activity that is designed to make you "fruitful and multiply". So even if you have an abortion or an adoption proceeding, it doesn't change the reality that your body went through the biological process of incubating and birthing another life into the world. Nothing you do after that will negate the reality of motherhood. It's merely after-the-fact procedure.

THE BEST WAY TO AVOID UNWANTED PREGNANCY IS NOT TO ENGAGE IN RECKLESS SEX

"Who can do that?" you may ask. And the answer would be *"The person who cares enough about his or herself."*

If you want a baby right now, this minute in your life, then go ahead. Have at it.

If you want an STD or maybe sentence yourself to death with AIDS or HIV, by all means, go for it. On the other hand, if you want to enjoy your youth, get yourself together!

PERSONAL STORY

While I've never placed a baby up for adoption, I have experienced the trauma of an abortion. And let me tell you, there's nothing pleasant about it. Yes, I was able to escape the chains of motherhood at 18 and could continue being a young adult and pursue my dreams. But nothing will ever erase that part of my life, the moment I became a mother, though I had nothing to show for it.

The abortion was my mother's idea. Perhaps she felt I would be better off waiting until I married to have children. Or maybe she wanted me to be more secure as a person. Then again, she maybe didn't want to be the grandmother asked to babysit all the time. Who knows? In retrospect, I may have done the same thing in her shoes.

All I know is even at 18 I was scared and at a loss when I learned I was pregnant. I can only imagine the fear of a 15-year-old.

It's not easy to tell the world you had an abortion. I share this part of my life because I left a piece of myself there, in that moment. I was fragmented; and it was my own un-doing. Healing literally took decades.

Maybe my story will help you avoid this mistake. Teen pregnancy is a mistake that stays with you forever.

Though we never spoke of the abortion, it placed a strain on the relationship between my mother and me. It was like a quiet storm raging inside—clouds too full to rain; winds too raging to blow. I blamed her, and she blamed me.

I knew if I didn't find healing, I would sentence myself to a life of guilt. My healing came when I forgave myself and let it go. I also forgave my mother, though she really didn't do anything. The initial act was mine. Had I not engaged in reckless sex, none of it would have happened. Taking responsibility closed the door; forgiving me locked it; sharing the story threw away the key.

You can spare yourself this ordeal…

SEX IS NOT A GAME

Sex is not a game and shouldn't be played with. There's nothing carefree about it. The only carefree sex is between husband and wife.

Every media outlet promotes sex. Commercials; movies; TV shows; music; you name it. In spite of all that, you must understand that **sex is designed to create life.** If you indulge in sexual intercourse, it's perfectly natural for you to conceive a child. Believing anything else will cause you enormous disappointment and pain.

Sex is so natural and spontaneous that you may not be able to resist the urge when it rises. Certain conditions make it more difficult for you to say "no". In fact, you may even be the one to initiate the circumstances. **It's important to be in control of yourself at all times.**

Most guys won't have the discipline to say "no", so it's up to girls to draw a balance. After all, at 15, you'll be the one stuck with caring for the child on your own—.

What If Your Friend Has a Baby?

Something happens to the friendship when one friend has a baby. It just isn't the same anymore. All those fun days you used to spend at the mall; going to football games or spending Saturday afternoons doing each other's hair and nails—all those times are over. Your visits are now interrupted by the cries of a newborn.

She's no longer available for spontaneous trips to the library or an afternoon matinee. When you call her on Saturday afternoons, she's asleep because the baby kept her awake the night before. Even her mother appears rude and inconsiderate when she answers the phone. She, too, couldn't sleep. Cries and feedings throughout the night kept everyone awake. The whole house is tired and frustrated. The mother's tone on the phone is nothing personal.

Things will never be the same when your friend has a baby. The baby takes up all of her time now. And when she does have a free moment, she's trying to catch up on sleep she lost the night before. Do you tough it out or accept the reality and find another friend?

THE BABY TAKES UP ALL OF YOUR FRIEND'S TIME; NO TIME FOR ANYTHING EXCEPT THE BABY...

When you're too young for a baby, you'll have a doll in one arm and a baby in the other...

In some cases, a friend tries to talk the other friend into getting pregnant by bragging about how "great" it is to be a mother.

This is how the new mother pretends to be happy to have a baby. She tries to persuade another friend to get pregnant, so she doesn't feel so isolated. Though the two of you are very close, and have been friends since kindergarten, when one of you becomes pregnant and has a baby, the friendship suffers. It may even end altogether. After all, what do you have in common anymore? You certainly don't have a baby in common. And soon you will feel the pressure to be on the same page with your friend.

BIRDS OF A FEATHER...

You know the old saying. *"Birds of a feather flock together."* The two of you are best friends because you agree on most things. You like the same kind of guys; you both like to dress cool and smart; you're both cheerleaders; and you have the same philosophy about most issues you face. If you didn't have these things in common, you probably wouldn't be as close.

So...what do you think will happen next? The odds say you'll get pregnant because your best friend has a baby. That's usually how it works.

Neither of you have given any thought to what life would be like if the other wasn't available for all the fun stuff you're used to doing together. Then again, why would you? You're only 15! But now that your friend is in this new and scary part of life, you probably think this is how your life should be too. You think maybe you're supposed to have a baby too. Maybe it's that phase in your life when it's time for this to happen. WRONG!

You feel this way because your "best" friend got pregnant and had a baby; now you're feeling obligated to do the same thing. STOP IT! **If she's a true friend, she'll tell you NOT to have reckless, unprotected sex.**

YOU HAVE TO MOVE ON...

As hard as it may be, you have to accept the reality of things. You and your best friend will not have the same kind of friendship that you're used to. She is no longer a cheerleader because she became pregnant and had to give it up. Those afternoon walks in the park are over. Her schedule is unpredictable and revolves around the baby's needs. Are you going to stop being a fun-loving teenager because your friend can no longer enjoy these things with you?

At first, you may not know what to do.

For instance, you have to go over to her house all the time for visits, since it's difficult for her—having to bring a baby along. Then your visits are always interrupted by what the baby needs. And he needs a lot!

It's human nature to feel a sense of obligation to people you're close to. You feel what they feel. Their sadness becomes yours. Their problem becomes yours to solve. So seeing the helplessness of your best friend causes you to want to make it better.

She feels helpless, alone, and trapped. No 15-year-old knows the absolute struggle it is to care for an infant. Even parents with several children don't know what to do in every instance of parenthood. So a teenager is definitely confused! Your friend's helplessness is justified.

Her time is re-assigned. The only personal time she enjoys is when the baby is asleep. She isn't around people like before; her days are lonely now—despite having a baby, she's lonely for her old life, when she was young and free.

Confined to the house; on 24-hour call; youthfulness stripped away. This is your friend's life. Not only does she FEEL trapped...she IS TRAPPED! As bad as that sounds, it's true. She is trapped in the role of motherhood for life! **She's trapped; you're not. What are you going to do?**

If you want to enjoy the rest of your youth, then choose to learn; grow; laugh; and love YOU!

MOVING ON DOESN'T MEAN ABANDON FRIENDS

Your friend has a baby. Not you.

Her life has taken a totally different direction. The plans the two of you made about being roommates at college are cancelled. Trying out to compete in the cheerleading championships is a forsaken dream for her now. But you cannot abandon your dreams because your best friend can no longer pursue them with you.

This is why you have to move on, in terms of keeping your hopes and dreams for the future alive.

If you hang around the house with her and the baby all the time, you'll develop the same type of "motherhood" mentality. And your next project will be pregnancy.

Friendships are validated only when they can survive the test of situations. If your friend makes you feel bad because you're still free to enjoy the wonders of being young—and she's not, then you don't have a valid friendship.

If she's honest with you, admits regret for her mistake of indulging in sexual activity, and encourages you to go all the way and be all you can be…if she tells you that having sex is not worth it, if you're 15 and pregnant—then she's a true friend. And she knows that "moving on" means you have to live life according to your condition.

Her current condition is motherhood; your condition is being a 15-year-old sophomore who pays attention to what your parents tell you, and makes choices that you won't regret. That's your condition…right now anyway.

You can move on without abandoning your best friend. Things are different; you won't see or talk to her every day; but she knows nothing that happens can destroy your sisterhood. Lesson: *When life happens; you keep living it.*

Some teens become pregnant out of friendship and misplaced obligation. Their friend has a baby; and they feel the only way to remain friends and keep things the way they are between them is to get pregnant too.

So you have something like a "pregnant club" where the domino effect spirals out of control and the entire tenth grade is either pregnant or trying to get that way.

STOP IT!

Getting pregnant because a friend had a baby is not cool...

The fathers will be nowhere around. And you'll be at the Department of Human services seeking child support and government aid.

He's Scared and Confused

Young fathers. They are hopeless, spineless boys. They really are. And I don't mean that in a judgmental way. But tell them you're pregnant, and they are literally shaking in their sneakers! They're afraid. What do they know about being a father? All they know is sports and video games. Being a father at 15 doesn't factor into their psyche; nor should it factor into yours.

Girls mature earlier than boys. So, just because a girl feels some type of way doesn't mean the boy does.

Tell him you're pregnant and he'll disappear. He won't answer your calls; your texts; or your emails. You won't pass him in the halls at school anymore; he'll become a phantom—. He talked a good game when he was trying to talk you into sex. *"What are you afraid of? I thought cheerleaders were cooler than the plain girls. I have protection. It won't hurt."*

All that machoism dissipates with the "daddy" possibility.

27

HE KNOWS NOTHING ABOUT FATHERHOOD.

In many cases, he's still a little boy, sleeping on Sponge Bob sheets. He's 15 too! The fact that the two of you had sex and made a baby doesn't change that reality.

Both of you are too young to be responsible for a baby. The difference is he's showing his fear; you don't have time to show yours. You got too much responsibility. The baby will live at home with you and your parents. As the mother, your very nature calls you to action—young or not.

However, when the baby comes, his schedule won't change. He'll still have just as much time on his hands as before—playing video games and trying to talk someone else out of their pants. Sorry. It's what boys do.

Any form of escape he chooses is not enough to calm his fear. He's confused, you're confused; and now your parents are confused—wondering where they went wrong.

HE WILL NOT MARRY YOU

He's your boyfriend and the father of your child. But chances are he will not marry you. In reality, no level-headed parent pushes their 15-year-old to marry.

At 15, you have no resources; the mother usually drops out of school; the father runs the other way; so getting married at this point is impossible. And *shot-gun* weddings are totally ridiculous!

On the other hand, when both of you reach adulthood, and you want to get married, that's different. However, the marrying rate is slim to none for those who have babies in their teens.

These couples usually break up a short time after the baby is born. Demands prove to be too much for the young father. His attraction was probably in response to testosterone—not true feelings for you.

Having reckless sex is foolish!—at ANY age! **Getting pregnant at age 15 is a self-imposed life-sentence for both mother and father.** There are so many other cool things to do. You may not believe it; but **sex narrows you to one small space that will possibly confine you to a lifetime of responsibility.**

Tsk, tsk, tsk. You're a "girl in love," at 15; you want to "give him a son". Just know...there's no turning back once you cross over into the world of parenthood. It's for keeps.

You're 15! How many times do we have to say it?

Even if you're 21, having reckless sex IS NOT cool; it's not fashionable; it's an open door to STDs. Do you want an STD? If that's what you're after…then go for it…

…remember. What you do now…at this moment…will affect the rest of your life.

MARRIAGE IS EVERY GIRL'S FANTASY

Arguments vary on the subject of marriage and what impact it has on society, in terms of family unit. Many traditionalists hold fast to the sanctity of marriage, though they merely exist in an unhappy one. Nevertheless, marriage is every girl's fantasy.

Every study conducted by government and non-government agencies suggest children are more balanced and prepared for adult life when both parents are constants in their lives, while growing up. There are also unhealthy marriages that are contributed to adults who had fatherless childhoods. Either way, it's common practice—right or wrong—to blame society's dysfunction on the fatherless.

In spite of all that, marriage, in 2015, isn't viewed with the same regard as before. Therefore, if one or both partners decide they "don't want the red tape" of commitment, it's not necessarily because he or she does not love his or her partner.

More and more couples adapt to "common-law" marriage by living together; establishing a home together; and having children as husband and wife. They believe and argue that a marriage license is only a "piece of paper."

Nevertheless, marriage is the process by which two people agree to be legally bound to each other for the rest of their lives. Some people are frightened by that prospect. It's like they want to change their mind later, and don't want the legal hassle. To ease fears, something called a "pre-nup" (*prenuptial agreement*) was born.

Prenuptial agreement – *An agreement made by a couple before they marry, concerning the ownership of their respective assets, should the marriage fail.*

Why is all this information relevant? It's relevant because all of it pertains to *marriage*. Young girls need to know and be aware that there is more to marriage than white gowns, bouquets, and bridesmaids. The concept of marriage is not the fairy tale you grew up believing it to be.

WHY CAN'T TEENS JUST BE YOUNG?

Having been a teen myself, I remember times when it was hard to **just be young**. I was always saying or thinking *"I'll be glad when I get married so I can do such and such."* Or *"I'll be glad when I get grown so I can get my own place."* I don't remember ever saying "I'm glad I'm 14!"

I don't know why it was so hard for me to just be young. You know, just "be" in the moment and not miss the best part of growing up. That part is hard to figure out.

This *ready-to-be-grown* attitude affects all teens. They never find pleasure in the moment; it's always "I'll be glad when…" Well, what about now? Why do you have to be glad "when"? Is there something wrong with "now" that's keeping you from happiness?

That over-anticipation in teens probably won't ever change. No doubt, you won't even realize you had this attitude about growing up until you have teens of your own.

I think maybe it's the lure of seeing adults with the freedom to *do whatever they want*, whenever they want and not have to answer to anyone. Adults get to have a glass of wine at dinner; and seem to always want to tell you, "You're not old enough" to have any. Go figure…

Adults don't have a curfew; their dates last till the next day without consequences. And you say "Man, I can't wait!"

On the other hand, adults really don't see the need to have these conversations with their teens unless something happens on the subject. That doesn't say parents are bad. It just confirms that no one has all the answers—not even parents. *Besides, teens hate having serious conversations on sex topics.*

When parents have kids, they don't get a handbook of instructions. Raising kids and growing up are mostly *trial and error*. No one can say their way is the so-called *right* way to do it. We just do the best we can.

So, what does all this have to do with teens not appreciating their youth? How does it explain why they're not satisfied being young and free? Answer: **Because youth is freedom; and freedom is youth.** ("Youth", here, meaning teens and pre-teens)

WHAT ARE YOUTHS FREE FROM?

- Mortgage
- Taking care of family
- Medical and dental bills
- Providing food, clothing, shelter
- No kids!

Being a teen isn't so bad after all, is it? You find this out all too quickly when you rush ahead of your years, trying to be an adult; and do things that could possibly strip you of your youthful freedom. Believe me. You'll lose your care-free existence soon enough!

When girls become pregnant, critics are quick to blame the parents. But parents have been teenagers; and most will admit that they made bad choices, even when they understood the dangers. In other words, they knew better-- but still made risky choices, despite possible consequences! So blaming parents is a cop-out. Most kids know EXACTLY what they're doing when they have sex.

Teen Pregnancy Facts

This subject has been talked about and analyzed for decades. Organizations and agencies are ever seeking remedies for dealing with teen pregnancies. Despite sentiments, it's true that thousands of young girls become pregnant each year. Of that number, a large percentage of them have another child within two years. So this is by no means a useless conversation.

As such, this chapter is dedicated to specific data on teen pregnancy. It contains startling facts about American girls and teen pregnancy. Information in this section is of a more serious nature, in terms of official data. While some may scoff at the idea of *teen pregnancy* as being just another blasé topic, this data rebukes that position.

Teen pregnancy is a serious dilemma; and though it's not a new problem, it exacerbated over time. Teen sex is compounded by the threat of AIDS and other STDs. So even if girls don't become pregnant, they are at greater risk of contracting serious diseases that could render them unable to have children or laden with terminal illness.

11 FACTS ABOUT TEEN PREGNANCY

1. 3 in 10 teen American girls will get pregnant at least once before age 20. That's nearly 750,000 teen pregnancies each year.

2. More than 50% of teen mothers never graduate from high school. Parenthood is the leading cause of girls dropping out of high school.

3. About 25% of teen moms have a 2nd child within 24 months of their first baby.

4. Less than 2% of teen moms earn a college degree by age 30.

5. The United States has one of the highest teen pregnancy rates in the western industrialized world.

6. In 2008, the teen pregnancy rate among African-American and Hispanic teen girls, ages 15-19, was over two and a half times higher than the teen pregnancy rate among white teen girls of the same age group.

7. In 2011, the teen birthrate in the United States fell to the lowest level recorded in nearly 70 years of tracking teen childbearing.

8. 8 out of 10 teen dads don't marry the mother of their child.

9. A sexually active teen who doesn't use contraceptives has a 90% chance of becoming pregnant within a year.

10. More than half of all mothers on welfare had their first child as a teenager. In fact, two-thirds of families begun by a young, unmarried mother are poor.

11. Teens had fewer babies in 2010 than in any year since the mid-1940s.

Media outlets often glamorize teens in sexually suggestive situations, highlighting teen parenting as something to strive for. However, teens hardly ever see the painful reality of becoming parents too soon.

More and more teen girls, aged 15-19 years, give birth each year in the U.S. Having a child as a teenager is emotionally, physically, and financially draining for the mother, father, child, and the community. Everyone pays the price.

If you're a parent reading this, you're probably planning to stick one of these booklets in your son or daughter's Christmas stocking; or you'll give it as a birthday present.

However, if you're a teenager reading this section, you may have rolled your eyes in contempt or disbelief.

That's okay. It's perfectly natural to scoff at situations…
…until it happens to you.

The purpose for the Teen Survival Series is to help you avoid being one of the statistics.

- One way to guarantee falling into a trap is to say *"it will never happen to me."*

- You will always need the instruction you refuse

- Blaming someone else for your mistake is denial of personal responsibility

- If you're old enough to disobey instruction, you're old enough to pay the price

Numbers relating to teen pregnancy statistics are constantly changing. They increase or diminish; fluctuate. Various organizations study these trends in search of cause and effect, aiming to find ways to prevent as many teen pregnancies as possible—.

WHEN SHOULD GIRLS KNOW ABOUT MOTHERHOOD?

There is and always has been a fascination with motherhood; the pregnancy and birth process. How life begins, grows, and finally exits the womb still intrigues the mind, though we see pregnant mothers all the time.

Perhaps the fascination with motherhood and caring for babies develop in young girls as they continue to play with dolls. Having dolls that cry, wet their pants, and wiggle their arms and legs makes the experience more real. So *having* a baby becomes more real also, and doesn't involve any unpeasantries when done in balance.

Playing with dolls is different in the sense that you can put it away and don't have to pick it up again for days at a time. But, babies are living beings; demanding constant attention and cannot be left alone. Even when you are rest-broken and need to sleep, you can't. Your first and only obligation is to make sure the "live" baby's needs are met.

In one of our impromptu motherhood discussions, several of us shared an opinion on whether it's a good idea to teach toddlers about motherhood. For example, should mothers use the moment they give their little girls a doll, to simultaneously teach them that babies are real and it's best to have them when you get married? Since professionals believe children learn the most between ages two and five, is there any harm in teaching little girls about babies at the time they receive their dolls?

Naturally, opinions varied. Nevertheless, the notion opened new possibilities, in terms of taking steps to prevent teen pregnancy and school dropouts among young girls.

Why not use every instance with toddlers as a teaching moment? They're learning anyway; so why not seize the moment to chart a safer, happier course for them in life?

Teens usually look for someone to blame for their shortcomings and mistakes. Parents are often among those teens target to charge for their failures.

THINGS TEENS SAY TO BLAME OTHERS

- My mom never told me about this. She can't expect me to do what I don't know.

- She got pregnant when she was 17 and unmarried; so what did she expect?

- They knew I had a boyfriend. Why did they let me go on dates—knowing sex might happen?

- If she had accepted my boyfriend, this wouldn't have happened. We wouldn't have been sneaking around doing things we shouldn't.

Taking Responsibility

Everyone has to take responsibility for their actions… or their "inaction". NOT using instruction you received is not the parent's fault. Likewise, NOT giving teens the instruction they need to help them escape serious life consequences is not their fault. Each blaming the other is not productive. And it doesn't change anything.

Admitting a wrong is hard. Nevertheless, when you take ownership of your actions, it frees you from personal scrutiny. In other words, when you "try, convict, and forgive" yourself, you start the healing process and the power to move on.

Everyone has a bad choice in their past; no one can judge you—so stop living that bad choice over and over.

For parents, admitting that we got it wrong is difficult. We're supposed to be the protectors, guardians of our children's wellbeing. When something goes wrong in an area where we didn't prepare them; or didn't set the proper example…we have a hard time taking ownership of our errors—especially with our children. Being a failure is every parent's greatest fear.

For whatever reason, we don't discuss our fears as easily as we discuss our dreams and visions. Emotions, like fear and pain, are explored in therapy sessions. Perhaps if parent and teen could find a way to be emotionally transparent with each other, there would be greater results from therapy sessions.

Parents have various fears about life as it relates to their teens. And teens experience similar fears, relating to their parents.

FEARS PARENTS HAVE

- Losing a child to death or abduction
- Failing to makes kids independent thinkers
- Having a child beaten and raped
- Daughter battered by abusive boyfriend/husband
- Drug-addicted teen
- Teen falls victim to criminal lifestyle
- High-school dropout or run-away teen
- Daughter becoming a stripper

Fears are natural. The only way to prevent them from materializing is to safeguard against them through truthful discussion. For example, a parent who has gone through an abusive relationship protects her daughter from the same thing by sharing the story with the teen. Hiding information increases chances of repeating it.

A mother's instinct is to do what's best for her young. Sometimes she makes a mistake in that effort; because as we discussed earlier, *being a parent is trial and error.* Mother's may pretend certain painful events don't exist, in their efforts to protect their children from unpleasant memories—or out of fear that their kids will view them differently if they know the truth about certain mistakes.

Sometimes parents hide past mistakes they made during adolescence from their children, which become their worst mistake ever. **Teens will encounter all sorts of situations throughout life**, some of which they may not share with you if they think you're "perfect" and will be ashamed of them.

When parents make it appear that they never made a mistake growing up, teens will not share information about critical points in their life. **They will instead talk to others and be prone to negative influence.**

All of us are subject to error. Life is a learning journey, with unexpected twists and turns, with bridges out in places up ahead.

We're not responsible for the turns we don't know about. However, we are obligated to make the turns we know about. And give kids the opportunity to turn around by telling them the bridge is out.

If they keep going full speed anyway, it's not because they didn't know.

It's never easy to watch your teen go down the wrong path, you being helpless to turn them around.

Teens have fears that create devastating emotions because in the past, adults rushed to judge them rather than try to help guide them through their problem.

For this reason, teens also isolate themselves, choosing to go through their situation alone than be scolded prematurely.

FEARS TEENS HAVE

- Afraid of being a disappointment

- They have different dreams than what their parents have for them; afraid they won't measure up

- Afraid of dying young

- Afraid of parents or siblings dying

- Afraid of the future

- Don't want to be alcoholic like friends

- Afraid to say "no" to peers, for fear of being ridiculed

- Afraid to trust anyone, after being betrayed

- Afraid of failure

Though they are growing into young adults, teens are quite vulnerable. Many of them are victims of bullying or some other emotional pain that they never tell parents about.

Unfortunately, while in moments of hopelessness, many kids commit suicide.

Teenage years are fragile years. Like young tree lings, teens need propping up until they can stand on their own.

We must guide and protect all our teens; but teenage girls require special attention. They are more tender and prone to a more severe instance of trauma.

By nature, females are more emotional. They feel and experience every emotion more so than their male counterparts.

This is because females are born nurturers and must be able to relate to the emotions of those she nurtures. Therefore, she feels everything more intensely.

It's important that girls are ready for motherhood when it happens. Otherwise, life is unhappy and off-balance for mother and child.

When pregnancy is an unwanted surprise, young girls run the risk of long-lasting distress.

She turns out to be a high-school dropout; a single mother that she feels no man wants for a wife; she feels she has no prospects of a hopeful future. This downward idea severely limits her view of life.

In many cases, young mothers who drop out of school, turn to alcohol, drugs and prostitution to support her and the baby.

Alcohol dulls the senses. Too much of it and it becomes easier to be taken advantage of. Someone can also slip you a date-rape drug.

Moments to Avoid

Girls are easy targets at unchaperoned parties; where drinking, drugs and loud music are out of control. **Usually older guys host these parties; and seducing young girls is their purpose in life.** It's important to avoid these moments, no matter how much fun you think you'll miss. Young girls are not safe at parties with no chaperones.

Here's a story:

Connie likes this cute guy at school; he's a senior; she's a ninth grader. Her friend, Sadie, gets to go everywhere because her mother is an R.N.; her father is a security guard; and they both work nights.

Sadie's grandmother is the live-in guardian, who sleeps like a slab of concrete. No chance of her waking up after taking her meds. The moment Sadie hears snoring, she sneaks out of the house.

Naturally, Connie wishes she could hang out with her.

This is Sadie

Connie's mother doesn't really approve of her being friends with Sadie.

"That's a troubled child." Miss Highland said shaking her head in compassion. "Her parents work hard all night and sleeps all day; and won't know what she's up to until something bad happens. Then, it's too late. Poor girl."

Connie is quieter than usual. She's trying to figure out how to go to the absolute "coolest party of the year." She'll do whatever she has to do to be there.

"I just have to be there!" she told Sadie as they headed to cheerleading practice.

"Your mom will die first!" Sadie said wondering if Connie was really serious.

Connie was serious all right. She had already planned what she would wear. She had never slipped out of the house before; so her mother wouldn't take any precautions to stop her. She was going to that party if it killed her.

"Okay." Connie went over her plan with Sadie. "You'll throw pebbles at my window when you're outside. No big rocks! Just pebbles." She paused to make sure Sadie was listening. "Then you wait for me by the big tree just past the street light. Don't forget to bring treats for the neighbor's dog."

"I don't know, Connie." Sadie said reluctantly. "Your mom believes in making you do hard time when she punishes you. Remember last time? You couldn't do anything for two months—just because you were twelve minutes late getting home."

"I'm going to that party! I don't care if I'm grounded for a whole year!"

Sadie shrugged her shoulders, submitting to Connie's persistence.

It's Friday; the day of (the night of) the party. School was like sleepwalking. Hallways buzzed with anticipation. Kids talked about the party all day. Making mention of it while passing each other on the way to class.

"See ya' t'night, Rick."

"Yeah. See ya' t'night, Bo." Fellow football players exchanged quick confirmations on their way—one to science class and the other to an English exam.

It was Friday; no one really focused on work, not even teachers. Everyone was ready to unwind from the week's routine.

Connie daydreamed about going to the party. She was so enthralled with the prospect of sneaking out that possible consequences, if she was caught, never entered her mind. Miss Highland would never consent to Connie attending an unchaperoned senior party, which is why she didn't even bother to ask if she could go.

Instead, she planned a way to get out of the house. She just didn't consider what could go wrong while at the party.

Sadie was coming down the stairs from the music room. Connie walked in her direction as she exited the counselor's office. She had been keeping an eye on her eligibility for the gifted class. She was following up with her on progress.

The last bell rang; noise flooded the hallways; and the echo of lockers opening and closing signaled freedom.

"Hey, Sadie!" Connie shouted. "Wait for me by the water fountain. I got some news." Sadie nodded her head to say okay.

Meanwhile, the 'fantastic four'—as they're called—walked past Sadie, asking if she was still coming to the party. She answered, "For sure!" in her usual care-free manner.

"Sadie, was that Ryan, Ken, Jess, and Kyle?!"

"Yep." Sadie answered. "Sure was."

Connie rushed up to Sadie in the naïve way that was typical of her personality. Running and almost tripping over her own feet, Connie giggled.

"You remember our plan for tonight, right?"

"How many times you gonna ask me?" Sadie teased.

"I wanna make sure 'cause tonight's the night." Connie had decided.

No longer was she going to be the only one among her friends who couldn't go anywhere and do anything fun, without a chaperone.

She and her mother argued last month because Connie wanted to go on a weekend trip with her cousin, Brooke, and her fiancé.

"Brooke is twenty-two and you're fourteen!" Connie's mother chided, "Why is it a foursome? Are you supposed to be Chip's date on this weekend getaway?" Connie had stormed into her room and slammed the door. Miss Highland had a talk with Brooke and learned that it was Connie's idea to ask to go on the trip with them. That episode got her a month of grounded time.

She just came off of that punishment; and now she was doing the unthinkable to get herself right back into trouble.

It was clear to Miss Highland. Connie was going through a phase of wanting to grow up too fast. She hated doing things with kids her own age unless they were doing outlandish grownup things, like smoking cigarettes.

She was caught skipping school just three weeks after school started. The counselor discovered she was under tremendous peer pressure and couldn't bare another day of having her money taken, so she befriended them.

Connie felt the only way to keep the three sisters off her was to join them. The pressure finally ended when the three were expelled for stealing a teacher's purse. They never came back after the suspension period. It was rumored their mother sent them away.

No one missed them; Connie was cautiously optimistic, but glad to get back to her bouncy, normal self.

Overall, Connie was a delightful and fun fourteen-year-old; although, lately her behavior was bizarre and alarming.

Her friends liked her a lot; she occasionally did homework for them; and they occasionally lied to get her out of the house.

Connie's mother is the typical overbearing guardian who watches the news too much; and thinks she has to prevent her daughter from being a victim. Much of Connie's behavior is in response to her mom's paranoia.

"Connie!" Sadie whispered loudly outside her window. Tossing another pebble, she called again. "Connie! Come on. We have to go! You said you'd be ready!"

The porch light came on. Connie walked calmly out.

"What are you doing?" Sadie asked.

"I'm going to the party."

Sadie looked confused; and kept looking back to make sure Miss Highland wasn't chasing after them.

"Well...aren't you going to tell me?" Sadie urged Connie to tell her what happened.

"She sensed something was going on. So I just told her I wanted to go to the party; and if she kept treating me like a prisoner, I was gonna run away." Connie explained.

"What did she do—I mean say?"

"She just looked at me with tears filling her eyes. Then she told me that I will have to find out the hard way. And then I will understand that she was only trying to protect me." Connie talked about the moment with sentiment.

"She's right." Sadie interrupted. "Moms always know what they're talking about. They may not always know how to do things. But they always know what they're talking about."

"Maybe. I'm tired of her treating me like a china doll!" Connie added. "I know she means well. But a lot of what she's afraid of is never gonna happen." She stopped and looked at Sadie. "Okay. I don't wanna talk about it anymore. Let's go have some fun! It's legal this time."

They both laughed and hurried to the party, at the Calvert's, two blocks over. Connie's mom knows the family.

Sadie went to all the senior parties. She was only fifteen; but passed for eighteen easily. She was very advanced for her age; and the fact that she was sexually active was common knowledge among the guy circuit. Now she was bringing "fresh meat" to a party!

They walked up the sidewalk and around to the large patio area in the back. Hedges secured the privacy of activities; and served as cushion for the music. Lights were dimly lit; tea lights lined the pool and formed a nice border along the stone walkway.

"Hello." A strange voice spoke from a table in the shadows.

"Who said that?" Connie asked.

"Sounds like that new guy." Sadie whispered. "He's cute. Girls all around town are talking about him."

"Why are you whispering?"

"Cause you don't want guys to know you like them. They dog you out in front of everybody. You just follow my lead."

A tall, slender physique makes its way out of the shadows and into a dim shimmer of light. He was handsome alright. His hair was cool too. Connie was spellbound.

He could smell her innocence. Her eyes were empty of motive. All she wanted to do was be a grownup. He extended his hand to her. "Hi. I'm Chet Jacobs. My friends call me C.J."

"Hi." Connie forced out a response despite the lump in her throat. "My name is Connie. Nice to meet you."

"Want some punch?" he asked.

"Sure. I'll get it." Connie answered.

"No." Chet insisted. "Allow me to honor the most beautiful girl of the night. I'll be right back." His words were dripping with ooze. Connie felt special; like she was the only girl in the world. She had found her prince charming just like in the fairy tales!

"Here you go." Chet handed Connie a champagne glass of punch.

"Let's have a toast." Chet raised his glass to hers. "To new exploits..."

"... and new friends." Connie interrupted.

'New exploits'. That was a curious thing to say, Connie thought. But she soon dismissed it when Chet asked her to dance with him.

"I don't slow dance."

"Will you make an exception for me?" he asked in a voice typically used to talk to babies.

"I guess..."

He pulled her close; she buried her head in his chest. Midway the song, Connie began to feel sick and dizzy. Her body felt as heavy as stone. She had no control over her movements.

Everything went out of focus, fuzzy. Nothing was clear. She could hear voices, many voices. Sounds closed in on her; she became hot all over and collapsed in his arms.

Chet picked her up and took her upstairs, explaining that Connie had too much to drink.

"She just needs to lie down a minute." Chet explained. "Get me a cold towel."

Sadie was already upstairs with her boyfriend, Connor. He loved to play video games; the only way she could spend time with him was to learn to play the games he liked.

"What's wrong with Connie?" she asked, rushing to her side.

"Oh. It's nothing." Chet answered. "I don't think your friend is used to drinking." Sadie calmed down. "Oh."

"You go back to your date. I'll take care of her. She'll be okay in a minute." Sadie went back into the playroom with Connor and closed the door.

Chet went into the room with Connie. He stood over her, staring at her still, innocent frame. He locked the door and began taking off his pants. Connie started to move around, like she was coming out of whatever knocked her out.

"What are you doing?" she asked groggily.

"I wasted a beer on my trousers." Chet lied. "They have to dry."

"Oh." Connie answered, rousing up from the bed.

"Just lie down and relax. My slacks will be dry in a minute. Would you like some water?"

Connie remembered something her mother told her about drinking stuff other people bring you.

She knew something was slipped into her punch. It didn't knock her all the way out because she didn't drink it all. It tasted weird, perhaps because Connie isn't a drinker. When Chet turned his back, she had tossed the punch into the flower garden.

"Where's the bathroom?" Connie asked, straightening her clothes and hair.

"Through those doors, down the hall, to the left."

"Thanks." Connie replied. On her way down the hall, she knew she wasn't going back to the room. She would go into the bathroom and call her mom to pick her up. Sadie could take care of herself.

"Where's my purse?!" Connie thought to herself. She must have left it in the room with Chet. But she was determined not to go back in there. She asked a girl in the hallway to use her phone, explaining that hers was dead.

As calm as possible, she called her mom and asked her to come get her. She didn't dare walk back home. It didn't matter that it was only a couple of blocks. All she could think about was almost becoming a rape victim.

A cute guy, she didn't know, had dropped a date-rape drug into her punch. He had flattered her into letting down her guard. For a moment she resisted all the teaching and warning her mother had taught her.

She could hear it plain as day. "Don't drink anything anyone gives you." Her mother told her. "Never turn your back on your drink. It only takes a second for someone to drop drugs into it."

"Are you alright, Connie?" her mother asked.

"Yes, mom. I just wanna go home. And I don't wanna walk. Will you pick me up?"

"I'll be there in a minute, honey."

"Mom…"

"Yes…"

"I love you."

"Love you too, Connie. Be waiting. I'm on my way."

"Thank you." Connie handed the phone back to its owner and began making her way to the stairway.

"Sneaking out on me?" Chet asked.

"No." Connie was confident. "I feel funny. Something made me dizzy. So I'm going home."

"Do you have a ride?" Chet was still trying to catch the fly in his net.

Squaring her shoulders and looking him in the eye, Connie answered, "Yes, I have a ride. My mom is taking me to the hospital for a tox-screen to see what's in my system."

Chet stumbled back into the room to quickly pull his pants on and grab his shoes. He left like a flash. Didn't even bother to say goodbye.

Connie walked proudly into the room to get her purse. She walked outside to wait for her mom, who pulled up right away.

"Thanks for coming to get me, mom."

"Where's Sadie? Are you sure you're alright?"

"Sadie's coming home later." Connie said. "Yes, mom. I'm fine, never better." She snuggled back in the comfort of the ride and felt thankful to have a mother who really looked out for her safety.

Connie had to have a near-drastic encounter before she came to her senses. She almost became a rape victim—all because she wants to grow up too fast.

Teen pregnancy is rooted in rebellion...

ABOUT THE AUTHOR

Peggy Hatchet James is an authentic writer who pens from the soul—a modern literary who appreciates the magic of words. Her passion for the wellbeing of young people spawns from her own troubled youth. Constantly seeking ways to prepare and strengthen teens for the future, James decided to develop a series of booklets under the umbrella of "Teen Survival".

"Each of us has a teenage past that's filled with mistakes. Likewise, each of us needed someone to remember and share parts of their own childhood as a roadmap to get us past devastation. We may not have followed the map all the time, but at least we would have had it to refer to—at crucial points."

--P. Hatchet

0 1341 1661128 3

CPSIA information can be obtained
at www.ICGtesting.com
Printed in the USA
FFOW01n1432011215
19179FF

9 781517 001919